It is in the national interest that personnel serving in the Armed Forces be protected in the realization and development of mora, spiritual, and religious values consistent with the religious beliefs of the individuals concerned. To this end, it is the duty of commanding officers in every echelon to develop to the highest degree the conditions and influences calculated to promote health, morals, and spiritual values of the personnel under their command.

—General George C. Marshall[1]

The headlines are rife with ethical breeches at the very top of our military structure. The New York Times names allegations against General Ward, Rear Admiral Gaouette, Brigadier General Sinclair, Colonel Johnson, and Air Force instructors to name a few and to highlight what appears to be a moral implosion in the ranks.[2] Earlier headlines about the role of religion in the military pointed to a different problem: "Air Force Sued Over Religion," "Air Force Academy Staff Found Promoting Religion," and "Naval Academy Urged to Drop Prayer" all showed up as national news.[3] There seems to be a disconnect—we are attempting to reduce or rid ourselves of the effects of religion as our incidents of moral indiscipline rise. Our governmental institutions seem to view many religious issues as separate from institutional concerns over morality and ethics. The back lash or result of the religious fouls called above has been explicit instruction codified in Air Force Doctrine that prohibits religious speech by leaders.

For the first time in history Air Force Instruction (AFI) 1-1 has been issued and includes paragraph: 2.11. Government Neutrality Regarding Religion. This paragraph states:

Leaders at all levels must balance constitutional protections for an individual's free exercise of religion or other personal beliefs and the constitutional prohibition against governmental establishment of religion. For example, they must avoid the actual or apparent use of their position to promote their personal religious beliefs to their subordinates or to extend preferential treatment for any religion. Commanders or supervisors who engage in such behavior may cause members to doubt their impartiality and objectivity. The potential result is a degradation of the unit's morale, good order, and discipline. Airmen, especially commanders and supervisors, must ensure that in exercising their right of religious free expression they do not degrade morale, good order, and discipline in the Air Force or degrade the trust and confidence that the public has in the United States Air Force.[4]

This stands in stark contrast to an earlier mandate:

All Chaplains are to perform divine service tomorrow, and on every succeeding Sunday, with their respective brigades and regiments, where the situation will possibility admit of it: And the commanding officers of corps are to see that they attend; themselves, with officers of all ranks, setting the example. The Commander in Chief expects an exact compliance with this order, and that it be observed in future as an invariable rule of practice. And every neglect will be considered not only a breach of orders, but a disregard to decency, virtue and religion.[5]

This was issued by General Washington as general orders of June 28, 1777.

Both orders are mandatory compliance orders. The first and most recent order asserts that compliance is mandatory for morale, good order, and discipline and has an underlying assumption that neutrality about God and religious teachings is conducive to those descriptions. The second order issued in our country's infancy claimed that compliance would be congruent with decency, virtue, and religion. In the modern era plagued by an epidemic in sexual abuse among military members, record-setting suicide events, and frequent senior leader ethical failures, it strikes a note of irony that religious behavior is the main thrust of brand new prohibitions codified by the former Chief of Staff of the Air Force. Certainly there is great concern on both sides of the issue of religious freedom in America and in our institutions, both private and governmental. This concern is in plain view on a billboard rented outside the Air Force Academy with former Air Force Chief of Staff General Schwartz's Religious Neutrality Memorandum written on the billboard. Essentially his memorandum states the same philosophy as AFI 1-1; however, it expounds more fully the idea and includes, "Therefore, I expect chaplains, not commanders, to notify Airmen of Chaplain Corps programs."[6]

Should the Air Force Instruction discourage religious speech by commanders? Is it based on legal necessity or on the desire to merely placate those who complained? Is the instruction really neutral as the title implies? Is this better for the morale of individuals and organizations? Will there be other implications with regards to Title 10 responsibilities of the Air Force officer? To find out, this paper will review the historical legal context, examine certain friction points within the AFI, analyze Title 10 responsibilities, and then offer a few recommendations.[7]

History of Separation of Church and State

Constitution and the First Amendment

Both the memorandum and AFI 1-1 claim constitutionality as a legal basis for the declarations. As can be readily seen, the climate surrounding religious freedom has changed dramatically since George Washington's 1777 General Orders. The First Amendment states, "Congress shall make no law respecting an establishment of religion or prohibiting the free exercise thereof."[8] A review of the congressional debates regarding the wording of the First Amendment clearly shows that our founders intended that no national church be established and that the Federal government would have no authority over religious matters.[9] James Madison proposed, "The civil rights of none shall be abridged on account of religious belief or worship, nor shall any national religion be established."[10] Joseph Story would write:

> We are not to attribute this [First Amendment] prohibition of a national religious establishment to an indifference to religion in general, and especially to Christianity. An attempt to level all religions and to make it a

matter of state policy to hold all in utter indifference would have created universal disapprobation if not universal indignation.[11]

It is unsurprising that "separation of church and state" is not found in the constitution or in any of the constitutional debates.[12] Sometimes termed a "misleading metaphor based on bad history" the concept of total separation has nonetheless gained traction today.[13] Since AFI 1-1 refers to the constitution twice in setting up the "Government Neutrality on Religion," it begs further analysis of the development of this concept.

Jefferson's Phrase

The "separation of church and state" phrase was first used by Thomas Jefferson in 1802 in a letter to the Danbury Baptists two days before he attended worship services in the US Capitol, a habit he continued throughout his presidency.[14] The Danbury Baptists, a religious minority, feared coercion from the government to support other Christian denominations besides their own and articulated that fear to the new president.[15] Jefferson assured them that the First Amendment erected a "wall of separation between church and state."[16] In this way he notified the group that the federal government was interdicted from religious jurisdiction. Never did he indicate that church should not or would not be influential over government or its institutions. Jefferson made this clear when he wrote:

> I consider the government of the United States as interdicted from intermeddling with religious institutions, their doctrines, discipline, or exercises. This results from the provision that no law shall be made respecting the establishment of religion or the free exercise thereof, but also from that which reserves to the states the powers not delegated to the United States. Certainly, no power to prescribe any religious exercise or to assume authority in any religious discipline has been delegated to the General Government. It must then rest with the States.[17]

4

This original understanding of a wall interdicting only the Federal Government (General Government) from presiding over or prescribing religious mandates was in harmony with jurisprudence at the time. Joseph Story wrote, "The whole power over the subject of religion is left exclusively to the State governments to be acted upon according to their own sense of justice and the State constitutions."[18] In keeping true to this interpretation of the First Amendment, the wall of separation phrase was not used in jurisprudence until the Supreme Court case of 1879, Reynolds v. United States.[19] Here it was recognized that the metaphor, as used, restricted the Federal Government *only* and the court had to rely on the normative character of good order in society, and not on religion, to restrict the practice of polygamy in the case at hand.[20]

The well-known Jeffersonian phrase and, more importantly, its modern day connotation does not reflect the attitude of our founding congress that passed the Northwest Ordinance.[21] That ordinance stated: "Religion, morality, and knowledge, being necessary to good government and the happiness of mankind, schools and the means of education shall forever be encouraged."[22] The state was to encourage religion for the sake of good government and human happiness.[23] From the founders' perspective, this could be construed neither as neutrality on the issue of religion nor as a violation of an establishment of religion. This ordinance was passed in 1787 by the same Congress that gave us our Constitution and was presided over by George Washington who stated,

> Of all the dispositions and habits which lead to political prosperity, Religion and morality are indispensable supports. In vain would that man claim the tribute of Patriotism, who should labour to subvert these great Pillars of human happiness, these firmest props of the duties of Men and citizens. The mere Politician, equally with the pious man, ought to respect and to cherish them.[24]

Today our society's understanding of church and state today is very different from that of the founders. Washington, in demonstrating the attitude of his day, argued for an indispensable relationship of religion and morality to political prosperity. He also believed that chaplains were necessary for discipline and morale in the Army.[25] This historic understanding found common acceptance culturally and in the U.S. judicial system through World War II. Following the war, an increasingly humanistic approach turned away from the historic legal understanding of church and state.[26] What Robert Bork described as the anti-establishment, anti-cultural revolution, and what Alan Bloom labeled as a crusade toward relativism, seems complete in institutional discourse and entrenched in many legal statutes.[27]

Consider the case of the Church of the Holy Trinity v. United States, 1892, United State Supreme Court case which examined an 1885 federal immigration law. The court stated, "No purpose of action against religion can be imputed to any legislation State or national, because this is a religious people." The court cited exhaustive historical precedence of the nation and its legal system. The brief outlined several court cases that recognized the state's encouragement of religion. It concluded, "These and many other matters which might be noticed, add a volume of unofficial declarations to the mass of organic utterances that this is a Christian nation."[28]

The courts began in earnest to turn away from that rendering of the constitution in Everson v. Board of Education of 1947.[29] The "impregnable wall" of separation was to make its way into the common metaphor of constitutional understanding from 1962's Engel v. Vital onward.[30] The Vital case was the first case prohibiting school prayer on the grounds of the "wall of separation," turning away from more than one hundred years of opposite practice and precedence.

Many legal and historical scholars today seek to document a far different U.S. history, where founders were largely a-religious and devoted to ensuring absolute religious neutrality in all government. Steven Green argues that the founders were influenced first and foremost by enlightenment rationality.[31] Noll, Hatch, and Marsden claim that the founders may have participated in a Christian culture, but that they approached government with liberal ideals.[32] Joseph Ellis writes that Washington led the republic based on deist traditions, not religious faith.[33] As the preceding review has shown, these perspectives can be problematic regarding both the lives of the founders and the original intent of the constitution.

The Change in Constitutional Understanding

But how much should original intent be weighted in today's courts? Does original intent of the founders have any legitimate argument for constitutionality? According to Richard H. Kohn in, "The Constitution and National Security: The Intent of the Framers," original intent cannot and should not be used as a legal framework.[34] To support his claim, Kohn uses Supreme Court Justice William Brennan's assertion that the constitution is obscure in its meaning and that it needed interpretation and coercion by the state to become law. Kohn quotes Brennan: "The genius of the Constitution rests not in any static meaning it might have had in a world that is dead and gone, but in the adaptability of its great principles to cope with current programs and current needs."[35] Although this attitude has become popular, the court has still recognized original intent as solid jurisprudence.[36]

It is important to mention the significant numbers of scholars who do hold to a "living constitution" framework and depart from original intent in the process. Supreme Court Justice Ruth Bade Ginsberg says that the constitution allows for very broad interpretation.[37] Steven Green sees the "Second Disestablishment" of religion in the 1800s as proof of an evolving Constitution, which continues to this day.[38] Don Gooding quotes Thomas Jefferson, "Laws and institutions must go hand in hand with the progress of the human mind."[39]

Against the "living constitution" perspective, Jefferson himself instructed Supreme Court Justice William Johnson: "On every question of construction carry ourselves back to the time when the Constitution was adopted, recollect the spirit manifested in the debates, and instead of trying what meaning may be squeezed out of the text, or invented against it, conform to the probable one in which it was passed."[40] In 1792, Justice James Wilson declared, "The first and governing maxim in the interpretation of a statute is to discover the meaning of those who made it."[41] In 1833, Justice Joseph Story stated, "The first and fundamental rule in the interpretation of all instruments is to construe them according to the sense of the terms and the intention of the parties."[42] Here we find a rich correspondence with James Madison's view:

> I entirely concur in the propriety of resorting to the sense in which the Constitution was accepted and ratified by the nation. In that sense alone it is the legitimate Constitution. . . . What a metamorphosis would be produced in the code of law if all its ancient phraseology were to be taken in its modern sense.[43]

This metamorphosis did eventually take place by the time Justice Brennan commented on the 'obscurity' of the constitution, debasing original intent in favor of modern day interpretations of constitutionality. Justice Brennan's idea of a "world that is dead and gone" dismisses the founder's principles intended for enduring application.

Some modern day justices are more comfortable with original intent. Justice Robert Bork, long time constitutional law professor at Yale, in his 385 page treatise on original intent philosophy, simply concluded, "In truth, only the approach of original understanding meets the criteria that any theory of constitutional adjudication must meet in order to possess democratic legitimacy. Only that approach is consonant with the design of the American Republic."[44]

Still, one man's subversion of the constitution may be another man's bulwark of freedom for the needs of a new day. Such progressive perspectives frequently reject concepts of America's exceptionalism, its religious heritage, and the idea that religion was vital to the founding of our Republic. Both sides might agree that one unique idea of the American experiment was limited government ruled by consent of a self-constrained people.[45]

Although the role of religion in government is highly controverted today, an honest historical review will show an earlier continuity. Noah Webster stated unequivocally, "The Christian religion, in its purity, is the basis, or rather the source of all genuine freedom in government. . . . And I am persuaded that no civil government of a republican form can exist and be durable in which the principles of that religion have not a controlling influence."[46]

John Witherspoon, signer of the Constitution, President of Princeton College:

He is the best friend to American liberty who is the most sincere and active in promoting true and undefiled religion, and who sets himself with the greatest firmness to bear down profanity and immorality of every kind. Whoever is an avowed enemy of God, I scruple not to call him an enemy to his country.[47]

Robert Winthrop asserted, "Men, in a word, must necessarily be controlled either by a power within them or by a power without them; either by the Word of God or by the strong arm of man; either by the Bible or by the bayonet."[48] Author Rousas John

Rushdoony warns of America's social direction away from her roots. He writes in his

book, *Law and Liberty*, "All law is based upon morality, and morality is itself based upon

religion. Therefore, when the religion of a people is weakened, so also is its morality

undermined. The result is a progressive collapse of law and order, and the breakdown

of society."[49]

If the above historical review seems arcane, it is nonetheless foundational for

understanding the tensions that exist in current questions of church-state and military-

civilian relations. It is thus relevant for understanding the current legal framework in

today's Air Force. Much of that framework deals with the government's current position

on neutrality towards religion.

Two Friction Points within the AFI

Government Neutrality Regarding Religion

The name of the paragraph under analysis in AFI 1-1 is entitled 2.11 Government

Neutrality Regarding Religion. As the name implies, it asserts that the paragraph and

instruction meet a legal test of neutrality. The modern foundational framework for

governmental neutrality with regards to religion is explained in McCreary County v.

ACLU of Kentucky, 2005, Walz v. Tax Commission, 1970, and Epperson v. Arkansas,

1968.[50] Essentially, the state is said to maintain neutrality between religion and non-

religion.

Although the concept of neutrality has been codified in constitutional case law, it

has been inconsistently applied. Examples of such inconsistencies are the court

upholding opening prayer for the Nebraska legislative session because such a practice

is "deeply embedded in the history and tradition of this country."[51] The court relied on the historical record of Congress (implying original intent) in their decision and documented that the same week Congress reached agreement on the Bill of Rights' language (approving the anti-establishment clause of the First Amendment), the legislative body also authorized paid legislative chaplains who opened up each session of congress with prayer. The Court's original deduction here is that the words of Fisher Ames, who penned the First Amendment, did not preclude religious influence and practice in government.[52] Later, this became only tradition in the eyes of the court.

The definition of religion given in United States v. Seeger by Air Force Instruction 36-2706 lends itself to unclear standards between religion and non-religion. That definition states, "A personal set or institutionalized system of attitudes, moral or ethical beliefs and practices held with the strength of traditional religious views, characterized by ardor and faith and generally evidenced through specific religious observances."[53] The courts, in a few cases, have even ruled that atheism, humanism and non-religion are categorized under the First Amendment religious clauses.[54] This definition and recognition by the court has led such notable Justices as William Rehnquist to say that the court's position on religion is "neither principled nor unified."[55]

Neutrality, although a lofty goal, may not even be possible in the AFI under examination. For instance, does the AFI 1-1 contain any prohibition against commanders telling their subordinates that they do not believe in the chaplain's programs? Does it prohibit the evangelizing or proselytizing atheist from telling his subordinates that he does not believe in God and therefore they should not feel they need to believe either? Because this is not the background within which the AFI prohibition arose, it is unlikely that that was a concern. Many might argue that the above statements may be covered by general prohibitions regarding good order and discipline. Why then a special statute specifying religious speech (and that only) as possibly demoralizing? Laws or policy in the government need to be "content neutral." Governmental action targeting religion or religious speech is generally prohibited.[56] According to current case law, in order for a policy or law to be considered religiously neutral, it usually cannot target religion or religious speech by itself without some "compelling governmental interest."[57] When free speech claims come into conflict with the government's prohibition against the "establishment clause" in religious cases, the basis for decision many times rests upon tests of "coercion" or upon whether or not the speaker is thought to be in an "official capacity." Still, one might argue the same thing regarding anti-religious speech that has not been specifically prohibited.

When looking at this friction and using an "official capacity" ruling, the court will determine whether the employee endorsing religion by engaging in the religious speech is reasonably perceived by an objective listener as acting in an individual or private capacity, or in an official capacity and thereby coercing or endorsing religion.[58] Using this precedent, the Air Force had previously issued Air Force Interim Guidelines which instructed supervisors about their "responsibility to ensure their words and actions cannot reasonably be construed as . . . official endorsement" of religion.[59] These guidelines are also in contrast to the tradition of invocations at official military functions.

The Air Force Interim Guidelines allow for non-denominational prayer at "military ceremonies or events of special importance" as long as its primary purpose is "not the advancement of religious beliefs."[60] When held up against Wallace v. Jaffree where a moment of silence in public schools was prohibited because it had a "religious purpose,"

12

the non-denominational prayer rulings indicate that our present religious freedoms and anti-establishment rulings are on unstable ground.[61] Other religious "holdovers" from our religious culture and heritage have been hard for the courts to dismiss even under their current "neutral" ruling construct. Military chaplains have existed continually since prior to the revolutionary war in America. The First Continental Congress authorized military chaplains and provided for their compensation.[62] Thus our military religious history goes back to the nation's very beginning. Therefore, it is not hard to conceive of General Washington's general order during the Revolutionary War requiring all officers and soldiers to pray and fast on 17 May 1776. That order was backed by the Continental Congress' order to observe that day in "fasting, humiliation and prayer, humbly to supplicate the mercy of Almighty God."[63] Such an order would be outlawed under our current policy. Truly, the courts goal of neutrality between religion and non-religion has been difficult to consistently apply and has led to much confusion about First Amendment protections. So much has been made out of neutrality (which dissenting court opinions have called hostility toward religion) that it is easy to understand why so many do not think that religious speech and freedoms enjoy any special protection under our constitution.[64]

The concept of holding religious freedoms in no higher regard than non-religious freedoms was proposed by the Obama Administration and recently taken to the Supreme Court. Their argument lost in a 9-0 ruling.[65] The administration's lawyers took the position that there should be no "ministerial exception" on religious-freedom grounds, for employers in religious institutions, from federal anti-discrimination laws. Church schools and other religious institutions, they argued, have only as much

13

protection as non-religious groups do on "freedom of association" grounds. This was an assumption that the religion clause of the First Amendment added no ground whatsoever for a unique religious freedom claim. The Supreme Court thought the Obama Justice Department's view was "remarkable," "untenable," and "hard to square with the text of the First Amendment itself."[66] In other words, trying to impose more freedoms for non-religious views than religious views is completely adverse to the founder's vision, intent, and even the text itself and therefore void of any constitutional support. That said, this has not been the consistent understanding by our court system to date which easily leads to the administration's confusing position.

For example, public schools in New York can display Jewish and Islamic holiday symbols but are banned from displaying Christian symbols.[67] Certainly the court has defined neutrality in a way that acquiesces to one side of the argument about church and state and has served to embolden more challenges to any existing form of religious practice or speech in public. Attempting to wade through the inconsistencies and confusion of court rulings, the Judge Advocate General's School has issued helpful guidance in *The Military Commander and the Law* as a desk book reference. This reference states:

> Religious expression cannot be singled out for special restrictions not applicable to non-religious speech. Stated somewhat differently, expression cannot be restricted just because it involves religion. Any restriction would have to be based on generally applicable, content-neutral factors such as disruption to mission or adverse impact on good order and discipline. Religion-related restrictions would be appropriate if the expression could reasonably be regarded as suggesting Air Force endorsement of religion, superiors forcing subordinates to participate, listen, etc. Similarly, "evangelizing" (sharing one's faith) and "proselytizing" (inducing someone to convert to one's faith or cause) are free exercises of religion and cannot be singled out for special restrictions not applicable to non-religious speech. For example just as it is not wrong

14

to share one's passion for sports there is nothing wrong with an Airman sharing his/her faith or inviting another co-worker to attend his/her place of worship. The active, interpersonal nature of evangelizing or proselytizing, however, makes it more likely (than display of religious items) to affect mission accomplishment and good order and discipline.[68]

The above raises the question as to whether the AFI prohibition will stand the test of future legal challenges and reviews, or whether it will be judged as an overreaching policy that attempted to remove all risk by removing any related exercise of judgment from the commander. Proselytizing is indeed active and interpersonal but so might be talking about politics or the nature of the war we are engaged in presently. Is it so much the nature of religious speech that has caused the focus or is it about the nature of the objections? Organizations such as the American Civil Liberty Union (ACLU; listed in numerous church and state cases) frequently attack in court the public exercise of religion, but do not engage over other moral offenses such as pornography. Today's environment does not prohibit the students of our public schools from wearing shirts that portray "the butcher of La Cabana" (Che Guevara) but disallows the showing of religious symbols on clothes worn to school.[69] Our legal environment is admittedly unlikely to reverse itself; so it behooves commanders to understand not only the prohibitions but also their rights and the rights of their subordinates and coworkers. A confused or hostile legal environment should not determine a commander's options. Rather, a commander should judge whether or not the practicing of one's religion would indeed affect mission accomplishment, morale, good order and discipline according to the AFI standard. The default is to approve requests for religious accommodation subject only to the limitations of military necessity.[70]

Morale

In the Air Force profession, where core values are "Integrity First," "Service Before Self," and "Excellence in All We Do," morale is not only important, it is essential.[71] While General Patton may have stated that some did not run because "we were more afraid of our consciences than we were of the enemy," morale has been, in every era of warfare, desperately sought after and tenaciously held onto when obtained. Morale is defined as confidence and zeal in the face of hardship and challenge. Because it is an emotion, it is subjective. It is reliant on individual feelings and their perceptions about their sense of belonging and the trust they hold in their organization. It is synonymous with esprit de corps. Clearly an individual with high morale feels included and valuable to the organization and enjoys a certain trust about that organization.

Unexpectedly perhaps, a connection has been found between the morale of individuals and their religiosity. In a recent study, called the Army's Excellence in Character, Ethics, and Leadership survey (EXCEL), the data found a high correlation between one's spirituality and one's resiliency, emotional stability, and positive effectivity.[72] Positive effectivity, as named in the study, speaks directly to morale and one's perceptions of contribution and worth as valued by the organization. The study indicates that those with stronger spiritual fitness have a higher perception of positive effectivity. The study drew a high correlation between a "hopeful outlook" and one's spirituality.[73] The EXCEL study shows that spirituality is experienced through religious identification. This may be an unpopular finding with modern authors who try to avoid the religious connection with spirituality under our current political and judicial environmental. Even though religion is not named in the definition of spirituality in the

Chairman's Joint Chiefs of Staff Instruction on Total Force Fitness, it is alluded to as "concepts of a higher order."[74] Such articles on spiritual fitness can achieve at best partial success with extensive emphasis on the spiritual side of the warrior with little, if any, reference to religion.[75] If religious talk is to be discouraged within the organization, does that assume that it is unimportant and has no links to the morale of the individual members? The EXCEL study indicates otherwise.

Morale and Marginalization

Excluding or undervaluing airmen would be a recipe for destroying the morale in a unit. This would also breed lack of trust in the organization. When one's values and deeply held beliefs are not welcome in open dialogue, or the public expression of those tenets are stated as being subversive to good order and discipline, it would seem obvious that morale would suffer. Although non-practitioners of religion might feel no effects, those with religious convictions might feel oppressed. The marginalization of religious members is recognized as a possibility in the *Air Force Law Review*.[76] Policy that might tend to marginalize any service member is problematic.

Edward Schein, in *The Corporate Culture Survival Guide*, theorizes that core beliefs of an organization can be pictured as a pyramid. According to Schein, organizational members uphold values and conform to norms because their underlying assumptions nurture and support those norms. The norms and values, in turn, encourage activities that produce surface-level artifacts. All one can observe about organizations or people are the artifacts at the top of the pyramid. The remainder of the pyramid is unobserved and lies beneath the surface.[77] Because our society is full of these artifacts, we can detect what some of these norms and values are beneath the surface and may even be able to speculate on what some of the underlying assumptions are as well.

The military is similar. Our artifacts point to underlying assumptions, deep down, away from casual observation. Headstones with engraved religious symbols in our national military cemeteries are artifacts pointing to underlying assumptions.

Schein also documents that organizations take actions to reinforce behaviors that conform to norms and values. Those actions are called embedding mechanisms. The fact that General George Washington insisted on chaplains in units and that they remain to this day, are embedding mechanisms.

Efforts which attack artifacts and embedding mechanisms are actually efforts against underlying norms and values. Efforts to remove certain offending artifacts reveal a drastically different set of underlying assumptions. We have already visited some of the court cases that are on the front lines in this war against America's artifacts and values. If there are new rules or attitudes about what a commander can say with regards to religion—more precisely, that he should say nothing or nothing favorable—it reveals much more than 'new and improved' interpretations of the constitution. It reveals a change in basic underlying assumptions. It aims at changing institutional norms and values. The underlying assumption in question is about whether or not God exists and if He does, if He may be freely discussed in public. South Carolina once held in 1778 that "no person who denies the existence of a Supreme Being shall hold any office under this Constitution."[78] In Updegraph v. Commonwealth, 1824, the court opinion stated:

> No free government now exists in the world unless where Christianity is acknowledged and is the religion of the country. . . . Christianity is part of

the common law. . . . Its foundations are broad and strong and deep. . . . It is the purest system of morality . . . and only stable support of all human laws.[79]

We can understand what the court's answers were to those questions above at least in 1824. Likewise, the House Judiciary Committee report in 1853 indicates:

[Religion] must be considered as the foundation on which the whole structure rests. . . . In this age there is no substitute for Christianity; that, in its general principles, is the great conservative element on which we must rely for the purity and permanence of free institutions. That was the religion of the founders of the republic, and they expected it to remain the religion of their descendents.[80]

Modern day decisions like 1985 Wallace v. Jaffree, where a one minute period of silence in Alabama schools was deemed unconstitutional, indicate the change in underlying assumptions by the court. The reason that the silence was called unconstitutional was not because silence itself is unconstitutional, but because the "intent" of the rule was religiously motivated and the judges ruled against that intent.[81] When the underlying assumptions of an organization are incongruent with or seen as hostile to those of the individual on such basic questions of life and its existence, morale will suffer. Incongruence between values and purpose is what makes leading in multicultural coalitions so challenging according to Angela Febbraro.[82] We can transpose this reasoning to our own organizations here at home. Sonia Roccas documents a study which discusses the detriment to individuals whose personal religious values conflict with group values.[83]

If the Air Force cultural narrative discourages religious speech, religious individuals could feel they are being marginalized. On the other side, if a majority of airmen agree with a non-religious or anti-religious institutional assumption, morale, at least for them, could improve. It is reasonable to expect friction between the two perceptions—in behavior, assumptions, and values.

Morale and the Practice of One's Faith

Especially for those in authority, but also for all service members, there can be a tension between loyalty to the service and loyalty to one's God, given the religious roots of the United States. This can be doubly problematic for Christians who understand evangelism as a mandate for adherents.[84] AFI 1-1 raises the question of whether acts of personal religious piety will be discouraged or forbidden in public, as potentially subversive to morale, good order, and discipline.

Morale and Prayer

The prohibition about religious referrals and the basis of "religious neutrality" for commanders would reasonably include such activities as public prayer. Prayer has traditionally been included in many military ceremonies, and central at critical junctures of government and society.[85] In the EXCEL study, prayer showed a strong correlation to one's hopeful outlook and a soldier's morale when returning from the war.[86] In a research paper entitled, "*Report on the Professional Military Judgment of Senior American Commanders (From 1775 to Present) Concerning the Crucial Importance of Official Prayer to the Morale and Well-Being of the American Military*," the Naval Aviation Foundation, Inc. and the Coalition of American Veterans, Inc. developed a case for unhindered prayer in the military. Their research demonstrated that commanders have consistently used prayer during the most pivotal moments in American history, both private and public, to bolster troop morale.[87] Ross and Smith, in *Under God*, document that General Washington used prayer and continued the Biblical philosophy that "the prayer of a righteous man availeth much," and even combined that with a

20

Biblical claim, "blessed is the nation who's God is the Lord" when he gave his public Thanksgiving Proclamation of prayer and fasting in 1789 to the fledgling nation.[88] Just prior to the bloody civil war battle at Gettysburg for the wheat field, the Irish Brigade knelt for chaplain-led prayer.[89]

Any military policy that would limit prayer to a private, "don't ask-don't tell" status would undercut the effective power of the practice.[90] Once religion is relegated to the private conscience, it is largely relegated to the irrelevant—both as a belief system and as a subject of serious public discourse—according to German Theologian, Dietrich Bonhoeffer.[91]

General Marshall advocated that morale came from "the religious fervor of the soul" and stated:

> It is the essential element of achieving military objectives, and is ignored at great peril, when soldiers hold only guns and orders, with no strength of virtue. . . . I look upon the spiritual life of the soldier as even more important than this physical equipment. . . .The soldier's heart, the soldier's spirit, the soldier's soul are everything. Unless the soldier's soul sustains him he cannot be relied on and will fail himself and his commander and his country in the end.[92]

Marshall's attitude embraces prayer as an avenue available to shore up the soldier's heart in times of crisis. The question becomes whether or not present day military leadership have made a case to defend such attitudes that were forged in great sacrifice. Or, have legal pressures made prayer more a problem than an empowerment?

Like George Washington before him, General Marshall connected virtue with spiritual welfare. Similarly, our founders connected religious spirituality with morality and virtue. *The Future of the Army Profession* makes the strong case for developing and maintaining a moral and virtuous character in the profession of arms.[93] Does building such character on a foundation of virtue ethics preclude strengthening a deeper foundation based in religion? Can a commander reference both foundations in fulfilling his or her Title 10 responsibilities?

US Title 10 Officer Responsibilities

The Commander as Moral Instructor

Good order and discipline in the Uniform Code of Military Justice (UCMJ) is thought to be the catch-all description of necessary behavior and can be subverted by numerous actions. Although all infractions are not specifically defined, Article 134 of the UCMJ threatens against, "any action that is against the prejudice of good order and discipline."[94] It has been claimed that over zealous proselytizers of religious faith have breeched this military standard, and that this led to AFI 1-1.[95]

The US Title 10 Code for officers and their role to play in the morale, welfare and moral practices of their subordinates is codified as follows:

All commanding officers and others in authority in the Air Force are required

1) to show in themselves a good example of virtue, honor, patriotism, and subordination;

2) to be vigilant in inspecting the conduct of all persons who are placed under their command;

3) to guard against and suppress all dissolute and immoral practices, and to correct, according to the laws and regulations of the Air Force, all persons who are guilty of them; and

4) to take all necessary and proper measures, under the laws, regulations and customs of the Air Force, to promote and safeguard the morale, the physical well-being and the general welfare of the officers and enlisted persons under their command or charge.[96]

The historical standards for interpreting and applying these standards have without doubt evolved. Is today's commander being asked to interpret these standards,

22

define them and teach them mandated, explicitly secular way? This could be akin to asking a world-class sprinter to train fledgling athletes who were struggling with their speed, while prohibiting the trainer from using the very training practices and workout regimens that had been key for the sprinter's success. Not only does this approach seem to lack effectiveness, but it would seem to disempower those who are deeply religious. In agreement with George Marshall as stated in our opening epigraph, Dr. James H. Toner notes, "It is not the principal task of the chaplain to be a command's moral educator.[97] Later in the same article he states,

> Moral failures by the troops—think of any recent military scandal—are at heart leadership failures. More often than not that means someone in command failed to teach moral responsibility, perhaps thinking very mistakenly that such teaching belonged to the chaplain, or to a certain church, or to the troops' parents and high school teachers. Much of that is true, by the way, but it nevertheless does not relieve commanders from setting the right example by deed and by word.

The Basis of Moral Judgment

Moral judgment is for most people related to religious foundation. In their 1988 objection to a California school curriculum mandate, the ACLU argued: "It is our position that teaching that monogamous, heterosexual intercourse within marriage as a traditional American value is an unconstitutional establishment of a religious doctrine. We believe [this bill] violates the First Amendment."[98] To their credit, the ACLU linked moral judgment to religious doctrine. Unsurprisingly, they then sought to have the related curriculum ruled unconstitutional.

The same tension exists in the profession of arms, if moral obligation and martial virtues are separated by fiat from any faith system. As we have already seen, this represents a sea change from the perspective of the founders and framers of our Constitution.

23

James McHenry, signer of the Constitution, Secretary of War, wrote:

The Holy Scriptures . . . can alone secure to society, order and peace, and to our courts of justice and constitution of government, purity, stability, and usefulness. In vain, without the Bible, we increase penal laws and draw entrenchments around our institutions. Bibles are strong entrenchments. Where they abound, men cannot pursue wicked courses.[99]

Similarly, Benjamin Rush, signer of the Declaration, stated, "Without this [religion] there can be no virtue, and without virtue there can be no liberty, and liberty is the object and life of all republican governments. Without the restraints of religion and social worship, men become savages."[100]

Dr. Martin Luther King Jr. appealed to this same traditional western idea when he stated:

How does one determine whether a law is just or unjust? A just law is a man-made code that squares with the moral law or the law of God. An unjust law is a code that is out of harmony with the moral law. To put it in the terms of St. Thomas Aquinas: An unjust law is a human law that is not rooted in eternal law and natural law. Any law that uplifts human personality is just. A law that degrades human personality is unjust. All statues [for example] are unjust because segregation destroys the soul and damages the personality.[101]

If this traditional understanding of moral standard is no longer acceptable, to what then may the commander turn? Has the commander been given adequate substitutes for determining, correcting, and training virtue and moral behavior in the command?

Universal Morality and Secular Value Theory

In contrast to the traditional view of moral standards related to divine law, the multicultural, modernist perspective sees morals as self-defined and culturally bound. The former conceives of eternal truths, the latter of secular standards. The relevant question is whether societies, organizations, and individuals can maintain high moral

24

standards without an underlying belief in an external absolute law of acceptable moral behavior. AFI 1-1 would seem to answer yes.

Dr. James H. Toner takes up the same position in his article, "*Educating for Exemplary Conduct,*" Dr. Toner advocates for the need of teaching virtue in today's environment of ethical downfalls and makes a good case that the failure of values on the battlefield may have strategic implications.[102] This teaching, however, he frames as completely separated from religious foundations.

Similarly, in a *Joint Force Quarterly* article, "Spiritual Fitness," authors Sweeney, Rhodes, and Boling defend spiritual fitness as being just as important as physical or mental fitness in the soldier, and they suggest ways to improve this by "connecting to something beyond one's self."[103] This connection is left up to individual choice, however, and leaves an institutional norm with no overarching moral foundation other than what the individual can summon.

With keen insight, most of these authors identify the breech in the institutional moral structure, and they suggest a plethora of ethical behavior and training. That said, they bypass studies that indicate spirituality positively correlates with several elements of ethical attitudes and intentions, as well as with emotional and physical well-being.[104]

Analyzing Secular or Universal Value System Theory

Much research has been done on the correlation between religiosity and values as cited in Sonia Roccas' *Religion and Value Systems.*[105] What complicates much of the results is the difficulty in assessing one's perception of values compared to one's actual values exhibited. Much of the data cannot be confirmed because the data measuring systems cannot distinguish between what values result from the religion as opposed to what religious choices are made as a result of one's autonomous values.

Also, hardly intelligible in data summaries are what values result from religious capital passed on from one's parents or other mentors etc. Even so, Sonia Roccas states that there are strong correlations between religiosity and values of self-transcendence and selfless type goals of conformity. In contrast, the data indicates non-religiosity correlates to more hedonistic values, tendencies for openness to change, and tendencies to act outside of the norm.[106] Will the discouragement of spontaneous religiosity in the institution encourage such hedonistic tendencies over time? One study even finds that an antagonistic relationship between church and state diminishes the effects of religious values across the culture.[107]

In the same article, Roccas cites numerous other studies. One such study done by Rokeach found that religious people "attributed relatively high importance to the values of family security, forgiveness, and obedience, while attributing relatively low importance to the values of pleasure and an exciting life."[108] If Roccas is right, one must ask if a shift to full secular values within military organizations is worth it, given an attendant projected shift from selfless to hedonistic behavior.

At a minimum, we must take seriously the distance we have traveled from the concepts of natural law and the moral foundations of our fledgling republic. William Blackstone, arguably the enduring authority on western legal philosophy in common law, advanced an understanding of natural law decisive for our nation's founding.[109] Peter Lillback, in *George Washington's Sacred Fire*, states the following:

> Blackstone wrote, "Thus when the Supreme Being formed the Universe, and created matter out of nothing, He impressed certain principles upon that matter, from which it can never depart, and without which it would cease to be." These principles to which Blackstone refers are "the Law of Nature," which was "coequal with mankind and dictated by God himself." Blackstone sees natural law as the will of God that can be discerned from

nature in general. But because of the sinfulness of man, because man's understanding was "full of ignorance and error," there was a need for revelation. The Bible was that revelation. "The doctrines thus delivered we call the revealed or divine law," Blackstone writes, "and they are to be found only in the Holy Scriptures." Thus, there is the law of nature (or natural law) and then there is the law known only by revelation as found in the Bible. Blackstone writes, "Upon these two foundations, the law of nature and the law of revelation, depend all human laws, that is to say, no human laws should be suffered to contradict these."[110]

Reframing natural law with secular, relative, multicultural values comes at a cost to the institution. Shifting foundations for law, regulation, and policy may not provide the solid structure for a secular curriculum for the commander or subordinate. This serves to prove that relativism is no standard at all but merely the altering of the norm to fit chosen behavior.[111]

Whether chosen behavior is founded on a dynamic concept of evolution, or on humanistic moral philosophy, or on multicultural values, the anchor of moral standards will lose its traditional western moorings of religion and the institutional ship will change azimuth. If institutional morality is divorced from the public practice of religion by an Air Force Instruction, changing standards and definitions of moral character or good order and discipline will result.[112]

Conclusion

Certainly the fact that the services are spending so much more time on ethics training for each service member is a testimony to our changing societal norms and the failure of those norms to uphold moral standards that are required by the profession of arms. Depending upon one's views, it is either ironic or fitting that the former Air Force Chief of Staff chose this time to codify secularist views and rule that a commander's discussion of spiritual welfare might degrade morale, good order and discipline.

We have examined the constitutional history of such religious tension in the public sphere. In discovering a changing legal structure and the inconsistency of application, Air Force policy may leap beyond what is truly constitutional. Certainly the neutrality of the new cultural statutes can be questioned. If the Air Force cultural environment is perceived as hostile to religion, morale may suffer. In this case, some in the organization may feel marginalized by institutional norms and values. Spontaneous actions of the religiously minded—to include acts of evangelism and prayer—may create conflict with expected behaviors.

Notwithstanding the new policy regarding religion, the officer is expected to carry out Title 10 responsibilities. These responsibilities include providing a virtuous example, guarding against and suppressing all dissolute and immoral practices, and ensuring correction according to the laws and regulations of the Air Force. What moral basis does the officer use in defining and carrying out these tasks? There may be a void of solid standard evaluation criteria. Although the secular ethics training based in multicultural values is commonplace today, this relativist perspective will continue to evolve with indeterminate results. If indeed we can find a secular, humanistic cure for the disease of immoral behavior, that cure has not yet been produced or consistently tried. We simply see the redefining of what behaviors are acceptable.

Because this modernist philosophy codified in our legal environment is progressive in nature and detached from the traditions and history of our founding, time will reveal the efficacy or inefficacy of this moral approach. Due to our history and current institutional social behavioral trends, it should have been recognized that the burden of proof for a changing standard remained with those advocating change.

Religious artifacts that have stood for centuries should have been given the benefit of any doubt, not assumed to be irrelevant. Unfortunately, today's reverse logic has meant that those advocating traditional western thought are asked to prove the reliability of a lost traditional system.

Religion is too important to be excluded from the table of military purpose, identity, and moral strength. In the words of one religiously minded senior officer as of late, "I just haven't encouraged young people to join the Air Force as I once did. It just isn't the same as when I joined and it will get much worse I'm afraid."[113] This statement was made in context of a discussion about religious faith and our military institutions. His statement reminds some of Germany's "brain drain" prior to the Second World War.[114] Can we anticipate a spiritual drain or even a moral character drain in the future by a segment of the profession who would apparently score consistently higher in EXCEL type spiritual fitness studies? Those scores purportedly correlated with moral courage, moral efficacy, embracing military values, soldier identification, physical resilience, emotional resilience, and positive effectiveness.[115]

Recommendation

Rely on the traditional views of moral substance and leave the instruction and safekeeping of that standard up to the commanders. After all, they are held responsible for all the myriad of infractions that may be "conduct unbecoming," in Article 133 or conduct "prejudicial to good order and discipline," in Article 134 of the UCMJ. The UCMJ has never defined every action that may lead to an infraction; why include religion separately? Why not rescind the problematic prohibition and hold people accountable? Poor judgment leading to offensive actions should not always invoke new legal restrictions that further reduce required judgment of commanders. Do we need new articles and UCMJ policy on adultery because so many senior leaders have breached the code? Let leaders lead and give command to commanders. Let them manage with prudence and capability. If they fail, relieve them.

As I write this, a sobering event has traumatized this nation at Sandy Hook Elementary School in Newtown, CT.[116] The dialogue surrounding the tragedy speaks volumes to the above questions. While most will debate possible solutions that address just the symptoms of a culture gripped in senseless evil, very few will target the root cause of human failure and the individual state of hopelessness that breeds a disdain for decency and moral order.

Endnotes

[1] S. W. Husted, *George C. Marshall: The Rubrics of Leadership* (Carlisle, PA: US Army War College Foundation Press, 2006), 179.

[2] Thom Shanker, "Concern Grows over Top Military Officers' Ethics," *New York Times*, November 13, 2012.

[3] "Air Force Sued Over Religion," *CBS NEWS Online*, Oct.6, 2005, http://www.cbsnews.com/2100-201_162-919947.html (accessed March 12, 2013); Laurie Goodsten, "Air Force Academy Staff Found Promoting Religion," *New York Times*, June 23, 2003; Alan Cooperman and David A. Fahrenthold, "Naval Academy Urged to Drop Prayer," *Washington Post*, June 25, 2005.

[4] U.S. Department of the Air Force, *Air Force Culture, Air Force Standards,* Air Force Instruction 1-1 (Washington, DC: U.S. Department of the Air Force, August 7, 2012), 2.11. According to the AFI Introduction: This Air Force Instruction (AFI) implements Air Force Policy Directive 1, Air Force Culture. The importance of the Air Force's mission and inherent responsibility to the Nation requires its members to adhere to higher standards than those expected in civilian life. As Airmen, we are proud of our high standards. Through self-discipline, we adhere to them, and we hold our fellow Airmen accountable to follow our standards. This instruction applies to all Air Force uniformed personnel (Active Duty, Air Force Reserve, and Air National Guard) and provides specific guidance on required standards of conduct, performance, and discipline. Where appropriate, this instruction makes reference to other instructions where more detailed standards may be found. This instruction is directive in nature and failure to adhere to the standards set out in this instruction can form the basis for adverse action under the Uniform Code of Military Justice (UCMJ). An example would be a dereliction of duty offense under Article 92.

[5] Tara Ross and Joseph C. Smith Jr., *Under God, George Washington and the Question of Church and State* (Dallas, TX: Spence Publishing Company, 2008), 35.

[6] Air Force Chief of Staff Norton A. Schwartz, "Maintaining Government Neutrality Regarding Religion," memorandum for All Major Commands, Washington, DC, September 1, 2011. http://forbes.house.gov/uploadedfiles/gen_schwartz_letter_religion_neutralilty.pdf (accessed February 22, 2013).

[7] A note here is in order in anticipation of an obvious objection to the paper's analysis. Only the Christian religion is dealt with here for several reasons. First, it only, is in any sense, the religion of our historical culture. Secondly, the Christian religion, the religion of our forefathers, is the foundation of our laws, morals, ethics, and mores. Last, because the majority of the American population identifies with the Christian religion, it alone is the target of the majority of the onslaught of lawsuits and poignantly was the target for those "offended" that led to the new Air Force Instruction under examination.

To give an historical example, the following excerpt is pulled from the House Judiciary Committee Report of 1853-1854: What is an establishment of religion? It must have a creed defining what a man must believe; it must have rites and ordinances which believers must observe; it must have ministers of defined qualifications to teach that doctrines and administer the rites; it must have tests for the submissive and administer the rites; it must have tests for the submissive and penalties for the nonconformist. There never was an established religion without all these. Had the people, during the Revolution, had a suspicion of any attempt to war against Christianity, that Revolution would have been strangled in its cradle. At the time of the adoption of the Constitution and the amendments, the universal sentiment was that Christianity should be encouraged, not any one sect [denomination]. Any attempt to level and discard all religion would have been viewed with universal indignation. . . . It [religion] must be considered as the foundation on which the whole structure rests. . . . In this age there is no substitute for Christianity; that, in its general principles, is the great conservative element on which we must rely for the purity and permanence of free institutions. That was the religion of the founders of the republic, and they expected it to remain the religion of their descendents. U.S. Congress, House of Representatives, 33rd Cong., 1st sess., 1853. (Washington, DC: A.O.P. Nicholson, 1854) 1, 6, 8-9.

[8] U.S. Constitution, First Amendment.

[9] *The Debates and Proceedings in the Congress of the United States* (Washington, DC: Gales and Seaton, 1834), Vol I, 451, James Madison, June 8, 1789, quoted in David Barton, *Original Intent, The Courts, Constitution, and Religion* (Aledo, TX: WallBuilder Press, 2008), 28.

[10] Ibid.

[11] Joseph Story, *A Familiar Exposition of the Constitution of the United States* (New York: Harper & Brothers, 1854), 259-261, quoted in Barton, *Original Intent,* 36. Joseph Story was the Founder of Harvard Law School; was called the "foremost of American legal writers" by the Dictionary of American Biography, and was nominated to the Supreme Court by President James Madison.

[12] M. Stanton Evans, *The Theme is Freedom: Religion, Politics, and the American Tradition* (Washington, DC: Regnery Publishing, 1994), 284.

[13] Engel v. Vitale, 370 U.S. 421, 445-446 (1962) (Stewart, J., dissenting). Wallace v. Jaffree, 472 U.S. 38, 92 (1985) (Rehnquist. J., dissenting); Baer v. Kolmorgen, 181 N.Y.S. 2d. 230, 237 (Sp. Ct. 1958).

[14] Actual phrase in letter to Danbury Baptists, January 1, 1802: "I contemplate with sovereign reverence that act of the whole American people which declared that their legislature should "make no law respecting an establishment of religion, or prohibiting the free exercise thereof," thus building a wall of separation between Church & State." Quoted in Ross and Smith, *Under God*, 116.

[15] Ibid., 119.

[16] Ibid., 122.

[17] Thomas Jefferson, "Memoir, Correspondence, and Miscellanies," *From the Papers of Thomas Jefferson*, ed. Thomas Jefferson Randolph (Boston: Gray and Bowen, 1830), Vol IV, 373, quoted in Evans, *The Theme Is Freedom*, 188.

[18] Joseph Story, *Commentaries on the Constitution of the United States* (Boston: Hilliard, Gray, and Co., 1833), Vol III, 383. Joseph Story was the Founder of Harvard Law School; was called the "foremost of American legal writers" by the Dictionary of American Biography, and was nominated to the Supreme Court by President James Madison.

[19] Ross and Smith, *Under God,* 122.

[20] Reynolds v. United States, 98 U.S. 1145, 165 (1878).

[21] The reader will be reminded that Thomas Jefferson was not present at the constitutional convention, the ratifying conventions, or the congress that authored the Bill of Rights, to include the First Amendment. As written by Ross and Smith, "Chief Justice William Rehnquist noted, Jefferson is a "less than ideal source of contemporary history as to the meaning of the Religion Clauses of the First Amendment." Ross and Smith, *Under God*, xviii.

[22] Edwin Meese III Chairman of Editorial Advisory Board, *The Heritage Guide to the Constitution* (Washington, DC: Regency Publishing, 2005), 302.

[23] In an address to Cooper Institute, NY in 1860, Lincoln made a brilliant speech in the famous ongoing debate with Senator Douglas. Senator Douglas had used original intent of the founding fathers as an argument for the continuation of slavery in Federal Territories and had asserted that the Federal Government did not have jurisdiction over local authorities to prohibit slavery in said territories. Abraham Lincoln took up the challenge and insisted that Douglas was correct in assuming that original intent of the constitutional framers should answer the constitutional question at hand. The soon-to-be President used the Northwest Ordinance of 1787 as proof that the framers themselves did not intend to extend slavery or prohibit the federal government from taking jurisdiction over the slavery question in the Northwestern territories. He affirmed that the ordinance that was passed in 1787 by several of the signers of the constitution was consistent with the signer's intent. He then went on to affirm that in 1789, when the Bill of Rights congress was in session, they ratified the Northwest Ordinance unanimously proving their intent on the constitutional question. It is of more interest to us to apply the same argument as Lincoln, on the same Ordinance, with regards to the Founding

Fathers original intent. The record affirms, as argued by possibly one of the greatest statesmen that America has produced, that the Northwest Ordinance contains the original understanding and intent of the founding generation and framers of the constitution with regards to all of the articles contained therein. John Grafton, ed., "Address at Cooper Institute, New York, Feb 27 1860," *Abraham Lincoln, Great Speeches* (New York: Dover Publications, 1991), 36.

[24] Meese, *The Heritage Guide to the Constitution*, 302.

[25] Ross and Smith, *Under God*, 5.

[26] Stephen L. Carter, *The Culture of Disbelief: How American Law and Politics Trivialize Religious Devotion* (New York: HarperCollins Publishers, 1993), 119.

[27] Robert H. Bork, *Slouching Towards Gomorrah, Modern Liberalism and the American Decline*, (New York, HarperCollins Publishers, Inc., 1996) 8; Robert H. Bork, *The Tempting of America, The Political Seduction of the Law* (New York: Simon and Schuster, 1990) 56; Alan Bloom, *The Closing of the American Mind* (New York: Simon and Schuster, 1987) 26.

[28] Church of the Holy Trinity v. United States, 143 U.S. 457, 458 (1892).

[29] Ross and Smith, *Under God*, 123.

[30] Engel v. Vitale, 370 U.S. 421 (1962). It is also noteworthy to emphasize that in the Vital 1962 case the Supreme Court acknowledged that they did not cite any precedent whatsoever. No such anti-Christian precedent existed in the previous years of Supreme Court rulings.

[31] Steven K. Green, JD, PhD., *Review of Drive Thru History America: Foundation of Character,* n.d. http://www.tfn.org/site/DocServer/DriveThru_Review.pdf?docID=2901 (accessed March 11, 2013).

[32] Mark Noll, Nathan Hatch, and George Marsden, *The Search for Christian America* (Colorado Springs: Helmers & Howard, 1989).

[33] Joseph J. Ellis, *His Excellency: George Washington* (New York: Random House, 2004).

[34] Richard H. Kohn, "The Constitution and National Security: The Intent of the Framers," *United States Military Under the Constitution of the United States 1789-1989* (New York: New York University Press, 1991), 62.

[35] Ibid.

[36] Marsh v. Chambers, 463 U.S. 783, 786 (1983).

[37] David Brody, "Constitution: Living Document or Original Intent," June 5, 2006. *US CBN News Online,* http://www.cbn.com/cbnnews/news/050801a.aspx (accessed March 12, 2013).

[38] Steven Green, *The Second Disestablishment: Church and State in Nineteenth-Century America* (Oxford: Oxford University Press, 2010).

[39] Robert Morgan Emerson, "A Living Constitution and Original Intent," *The Wall Street Journal*, November 9, 2007, http://online.wsj.com/article/SB119457845606187586.html (accessed March 12, 2013).

[40] Thomas Jefferson, *Memoir, Correspondence, and Miscellanies, From the Papers of Thomas Jefferson Vol. IV*, ed. Thomas Jefferson Randolph (Boston: Gray and Bowen, 1830), 373.

[41] James Wilson, *The Works of the Honourable James Wilson, Lectures on Law Delivered in the College of Philadelphia; Introductory Lecture: Of the Study of the Law in the United States Vol. I*, ed. Bird Wilson (Philadelphia: Bronson and Chauncey, 1804), 14. James Wilson was one of only six who signed both the Declaration of Independence and the Constitution, he was the second-most active member of the Constitutional Convention, speaking 168 times on the floor of the Convention; he was a law professor; he was nominated by President George Washington as an original Justice on the U.S. Supreme Court; and in 1792 he was co-author of America's first legal commentaries on the Constitution.

[42] Joseph Story, *Commentaries on the Constitution of the United States Vol. III* (Boston: Hilliard, Gray, and Company, 1833), 383. Joseph Story was the Founder of Harvard Law School; was called the "foremost of American legal writers" by the Dictionary of American Biography, and was nominated to the Supreme Court by President James Madison.

[43] James Madison, *The Writings of James Madison*, ed. Gaillard Hunt (New York: G. P. Putnam's Sons, 1910), Vol IX, 191.

[44] Bork, *The Tempting of America*, 143.

[45] Evans, *The Theme is Freedom*, 104.

[46] K. Alan Snyder, *Defining Noah Webster: Mind and Morals in the Early Republic* (New York: University Press of America, 1990), 253.

[47] John Witherspoon, *The Works of John Witherspoon, On the Truth of the Christian Religion* (Edinburgh: J. Ogle, 1815), Vol VIII, 33.

[48] Robert Winthrop, *Addresses and Speeches on Various Occasions* (Boston: Little, Brown 1852), 172. Robert Winthrop was a speaker of the U.S House and was a noted statesman alongside of John Quincy Adams and was contemporary with Daniel Webster.

[49] Rousas J. Rushdoony, *Law & Liberty* (Vallecito, CA: Ross House Books, 2009), back cover.

[50] McCreary County v. ACLU of Kentucky, 545 U.S. 844 (2005); Walz v. Tax Commission, 397 U.S. 664 (1970); Epperson v. Arkansas, 393 U.S. 97 (1968).

[51] Marsh v. Chambers, 463 U.S. 783, 786 (1983).

[52] *The Debates and Proceedings in the Congress of the United States* (Washington, DC: Gales & Seaton, 1834), 448-450.

[53] United States v. Seeger, 380 U.S. 163, 176 (1965); U.S. Department of the Air Force, *Military Equal Opportunity Program Attachment I*, Force Instruction 36-2706 (Washington, DC: U.S. Department of the Air Force, July 29 2004), 69-70.

[54] County of Allegheny v. ACLU, 492 U.S. 573, 590 (1989); Theriault v. Silber, 547 F.2d 1279 (5th Cir. 1977); Malnak v. Yogi, 440 F. Sup. 1284 287 (D.N.J. 1977); Grove v. Mead School District, 753,F.2d 1528, 1534 (9th Cir. 1985); Torcaso v. Watkins, 367 U.S. 488, 495, n. 11 (1961).

[55] Wallace v. Jaffree, 472 U.S. 38, 107 (1985), (Rehnquist, J., dissenting). Justice Rehnquist states in his dissent, "A State may lend to parochial school children geography textbooks that contain maps of the United States, but the State may not lend maps of the United States for use in geography class. A State may lend textbooks on American colonial history, but it may not lend a film of George Washington, or a film projector to show it in history class. A State may lend classroom workbooks, but may not lend workbooks in which the parochial school children write, thus rendering them nonreusable. A State may pay for bus transportation to religious schools but may not pay for bus transportation from the parochial school to the pubic zoo or natural history museum for a field trip. A State may pay for diagnostic services conducted in the parochial school but therapeutic services must be given in a different building; speech and hearing "services" conducted by the State inside the sectarian school are forbidden, but the State may conduct speech and hearing diagnostic testing inside the sectarian school. Exceptional parochial school students may receive counseling, but it must take place outside of the parochial school, such as in a trailer parked down the street. A State may give cash to a parochial school to pay for the administration of state-written tests and state ordered reporting services, but it may not provide funds for teacher-prepared test on secular subjects. Religious instruction may not be given in public school, but the public school may release students during the day for religion classes elsewhere, and may enforce attendance at those classes with its truancy laws." Quoted in Barton, *Original Intent*, 245.

Author's note: Neutrality rarely exists on either side of the question if at all. Those that sponsored the rental of the billboard to display the memo from General Schwartz are from the Military Religious Freedom Foundation. I do not think they would recognize any dilemma about ridding the Air Force of religious speech. Their website states, "The continued separation of church and state is the thin red line preventing our republic from devolving into a superstitious theocracy obsessed with fulfilling prophetic "End Times" eschatology. One has to wonder whether or not the safeguarding of the constitution by removal of religious connotations, doctrines, or beliefs from the Air Force Institution is the real motivating factor to their position. They may be motivated by their idea of the Christian religion being superstitious. Whether or not the Christian religion is superstitious is not the constitutional question, at least not framed publicly. Another description in his newsletter, website founder, Mikey Weinstein states, "…pervasive evangelical fundamentalist cancer spreading rapidly within the U.S. Military." And yet, in another segment he states, "those bible-thumping bigots." He outlines what he calls, "persistent exposure of their obscene anti-constitutional efforts." The question is not whether or not Mikey Weinstein read anything written by the founding fathers regarding the constitution while in law school. What is important is that the question of religious freedoms, establishment, and religious speech has been difficult for the courts to navigate and harder it seems for individuals on both sides of the issue. What complicates the subject is when those that are interested in the issue continue to cloak their dialogue in constitutional neutrality in attempt to give legitimacy to what may seem as a lack of religious tolerance to some or at least a disdain for America's 300 plus year heritage. This is the common environment today with regards to the question of religious freedom.

[56] Church of the kukumi Babalu Aye v. City of Hialeah, 508 U.S. 520, 532 (1993).

[57] David E. Fitzkee and Linell A. Letendre, "Religion in the Military: Navigating the Channel Between the Religion Clauses," *The Air Force Law Review*, 59 (2007): 1-71.

[58] Michael W. McConnell, State Action and the Supreme Court's Emerging Consensus on the Line Between Establishment and Private Religious Expression, 28 PEEP. L. REV. 681, 682 (2001); Santa Fe Independent School District v. Dow, 530 U.S. 290, 308 (2000), (noting the importance of the perceptions of an objective observer.); Lynch v. Donnelly, 465, U.S. 668, 690-93 (1984).

[59] U.S. Department of the Air Force, *Air Force Interim Guidelines* (Washington, DC: U. S. Department of the Air Force, 9 February 2006), supra note 26, paragraph 2E: and supra note 26, paragraph 4.

[60] Air Force Interim Guidelines, supra note 26, paragraph 2E: and supra note 26, paragraph 4. Non-sectarian prayer is usually understood as prayer that uses only generic names in addressing the divinity. Non-denominational prayer would be one that is indistinguishable between church denominations. The original Air Force Interim Guidelines used the phrase "non-sectarian" but chose to drop that phrase in their revised guidance in favor of non-denominational.

[61] Wallace v. Jaffree, 472 U.S. 38 (1985).

[62] Katcoff v. Marsh, 755 F.2d 223, 225 (2d Cir. 1984). The court has held that the military needs uniformed, credentialed, professional clergy (chaplains) based on government interest, the unique military environment, and the military mission, which requires religious support qualifications, knowledge, and skills. Government interest includes demonstrated history and legal authority, and the purpose to provide for the free exercise rights of service members without excessive legal entanglement.

[63] Ross and Smith, *Under God*, 142.

[64] Lee v. Weisman, 505 U.S. 57, 509 (1992), (Scalia, J., dissenting). The author encourages the reading of this modern day dissent to the court's anti-religious direction.

[65] Hosanna-Tabor Evangelical Lutheran Church and School v. Equal Employment Opportunity Commission, 10-559 (2012), quoted in Matthew J. Franck, "Individual, Community, and State: How to Think About Religious Freedom," *Imprimis*, 41, no. 9 (September 2012): 3.

[66] Ibid.

[67] Skoros v. City of New York, 437 F.3d 1 (2d Circuit 2006).

[68] *The Judge Advocate General's School, The Military Commander and the Law 2012, Workplace Religious Expression*, 246. http://www.afjag.af.mil/shared/media/document/AFD-120828-043.pdf (accessed February 28, 2013). Copies can also be found at The Judge

Advocate General's School, 150 Chennault Circle (Bldg 694),Maxwell Air Force Base, Alabama 36112-6418, (334) 953-2802 or DSN 493-2802.

[69] Harper v. Poway Unified School District, 445 F.3d 1166 (9th Circuit 2006).

[70] Department of Defense Instruction, *Accommodation of Religious Practices Within the Military Service* (Washington, DC: DoDI Number 1300.17, February 10, 2009), 2.

[71] U.S. Department of the Air Force, *Air Force Culture*, Air Force Instruction 1-1 (Washington, DC: U. S. Department of the Air Force, August 2012), 1.3.7. This section reads: 1.3. Core Values. The Air Force Core Values are Integrity First, Service Before Self, and Excellence In All We Do. Integrity is a character trait. It is the willingness to do what is right even when no one is looking. It is the moral compass, the inner voice; the voice of self-control; the basis for the trust that is essential in today's military. Service Before Self tells us that professional duties take precedence over personal desires. Excellence In All We Do directs us to develop a sustained passion for the continuous improvement and innovation that will propel the Air Force into a long-term, upward vector of accomplishment and performance. Our core values define our standards of conduct. Our standards of conduct define how Airmen should behave when interacting with others and when confronting challenges in the environment in which we live and work. (United States Air Force Core Values, 1 January 1997).

[72] COL Franklin Eric Wester, "Soldier Spirituality in a Combat Zone and Preliminary Findings about Correlations with Ethics and Resilience," *Journal of Healthcare, Science and the Humanities*, 1, no. 2 (2011), 67-86, http://www.usna.edu/ethics/publications/documents/JHSHVol1No2[1].pdf (accessed on March 6, 2013). Wester evaluates the results of a survey of U.S. Soldiers in the combat zone of Iraq collected in the summer 2009. Named the Army's Excellence in Character, Ethics, and Leadership (EXCEL) survey, it measured spirituality as one variable as a dimension of character among Soldiers.

[73] Ibid., 77.

[74] Chairman of the Joint Chiefs of Staff, *JCSI total force fitness framework – Spiritual fitness domain* (Washington, DC: U.S. Joint Chiefs of Staff, March 23, 2010): Enclosure B5.

[75] Colonel Patrick J. Sweeney, Dr. Jeffrey E. Rhodes, and Bruce Boling, "Spiritual Fitness, A Key Component of Total Force Fitness," *Joint Force Quarterly*, Issue 66 (3rd quarter 2012).

[76] Fitzkee and Letendre, "Religion in the Military," 1-71.

[77] Edward H. Schein, *The Corporate Culture Survival Guide* (San Francisco: Jossey Bass, 1999): 12, quoted in Stephen J. Gerras, Leonard Wong, and Charles D. Allen, *Organizational Culture: Applying A Hybrid Model to the U. S. Army*, Department of Command, Leadership and Management, *Selected Readings in Strategic Leadership, AY13* (Carlisle Barracks, PA: U.S. Army War College, November 2008), 203.

[78] Evans, *The Theme is Freedom*, 276.

[79] Updegraph v. Commonwealth, 11Serg. & Rawle 394 (PA. 1824).

[80] U.S. Congress, House, Judiciary Committee, *Reports of Committees of the House of Representatives Made During the First Session of the Thirty-Third Congress,* 33rd Cong., 1st sess., 1854 (Washington, DC: A.O.P. Nicholson, 1854), 1, 6, 8-9.

[81] Wallace v. Jaffree, 472 U.S. 38 (1985).

[82] Angela R. Febbraro, *"Leadership and Command," in RTO-TR-HRM-120- Multinational Military Operations and Intercultural Factors,* (Research and Technology Organization of NATO: November 2008), 3-1-3-13, quoted in Department of Command, Leadership, and Management, *Selective Readings in Strategic Thinking,* AY13 (Carlisle Barracks, PA: U.S. Army War College, August 2012), 307.

[83] Sonia Roccas, "Religion and Value Systems," *Journal of Social Issues,* 61, no. 4 (2005): 747-759.

[84] Matthew 28:19 Bible, American Standard Version of 1901 (ASV). "Go ye therefore, and make disciples of all the nations, baptizing them into the name of the Father and of the Son and of the Holy Spirit."

[85] Evans, *The Theme is Freedom,* 274.

[86] Wester, "Soldier Spirituality," 84.

[87] Admiral Thomas H. Moorer, U.S.N., (Ret.)., Vice Admiral Gerald E. Miller, U.S.N., (Ret.), and Rear Admiral C.A. Hill, U.S.N. (Ret.), *Report on the Professional Military Judgment of Senior American Commanders (From 1775 to Present) Concerning the Crucial Importance of Official Prayer to the Morale and Well-Being of the American Military* (Naval Aviation Foundation, and the Coalition of American Veterans, 2011). http://firstprinciplespress.org/newsite/wp-content/uploads/2011/10/REPORT-ON-THE-PROFESSIONAL-MILITARY-JUDGMENT-OF-SENIOR-AMERICAN-COMMANDERS-FROM-1775-TO-PRESENT-FPP-.pdf (accessed March 13, 2013).

[88] Ross and Smith, *Under God,* 215. Bible (ASV) James 5:15 The supplication of a righteous man availeth much in its working. Bible (ASV); Psalms 33:12 Blessed is the nation whose God is Jehovah, The people whom he hath chosen for his own inheritance.

[89] George C. Rable, *God's Almost Chosen Peoples, A Religious History of the American Civil War* (Chapel Hills, NC: University of North Carolina Press, 2010), 161.

[90] Lee v. Weisman, 505 U.S. 57, 509 (1992), (Scalia, J., dissenting).

[91] Eric Metaxas, *Bonhoeffer, Pastor, Martyr, Prophet, Spy* (Nashville, TN: Thomas Nelson, 2010) 155. Bonhoeffer was eventually executed for his resistance against Nazi Germany.

[92] Marshall, quoted in Moorer, Miller, and Hill, *Crucial Importance of Official Prayer,* ii.

[93] Don M. Snider, prj dir, Lloyd J. Matthews, ed., *The Future of the Army Profession* (New York, McGraw Hill Companies, 2005), 395.

[94] Uniform Code of Military Justice, Punitive Articles of the UCMJ: Article 134-General Article, http://usmilitary.about.com/od/punitivearticles/a/134.htm (accessed February 28, 2013).

[95] Fitzkee and Letendre, *Religion in the Military*, 1-71.

[96] Requirement of Exemplary Conduct, 10 US Code, sec. 8583 [Air Force] http://www.law.cornell.edu/uscode/text/10/8583 (accessed February 28, 2013).

[97] Dr James H. Toner, "Educating for Exemplary Conduct," *Air & Space Power Journal* (Spring 2006): http://www.airpower.maxwell.af.mil/airchronicles/apj/apj06/spr06/tner.html (accessed March 6, 2013).

[98] Barton, *Original Intent*, 72. A letter to Senator Newton Russell dated April 18, 1988 by the ACLU California Legislative Office.

[99] Bernard C. Steiner, *One Hundred and Ten Years of Bible Society Work in Maryland*, (Baltimore: Maryland Bible Society, 1921), 14.

[100] Benjamin Rush, "To American Farmers About to Settle in New Parts of the United States," "On the Mode of Education Proper in a Republic," *Essay, Literary, Moral and Philosophical* (Philadelphia: Thomas and Samuel Bradford, 1798), 8; Benjamin Rush, *Letters of Benjamin Rush*, ed. L. H. Butterfield (Princeton: American Philosophical Society, 1951), 1, 505.

[101] "Letter from Birmingham Jail" (16 April 1963), The Martin Luther King, Jr. Papers Project at Stanford University, http:///www.stanford.Edu/group/King/frequentdocs/Birmingham.pdf quoted in Dr James H. Toner, "Educating for Exemplary Conduct," *Air &Space Power Journal* (Spring 2006): http://www.airpower.maxwell.af.mil/airchronicles/apj/apj06/spr06/tner.html (accessed February 28, 2013).

[102] Dr James H. Toner, "Educating for Exemplary Conduct," *Air & Space Power Journal* (Spring 2006): http://www.airpower.maxwell.af.mil/airchronicles/apj/apj06/spr06/tner.html (accessed February 21, 2013).

[103] Colonel Patrick J. Sweeney, Dr. Jeffrey E. Rhodes, and Bruce Boling, "Spiritual Fitness, A Key Component of Total Force Fitness," *Joint Force Quarterly*, Issue 66 (3rd quarter 2012): 37.

[104] Wester, "Soldier Spirituality," 84.

[105] Sonia Roccas, "Religion and Value Systems," *Journal of Social Issues*, 61, no. 4 (2005): 747-759.

[106] Ibid.

[107] S. Roccas, and S.H. Schwartz, "Church-State Relations and the Associations of Religiosity with Values: A Study of Catholics in XIX Countries," *Cross-Cultural Research*, 31 (1997): 356-375.

[108] Roccas, "Religion and Value Systems," 747-759.

[109] Peter A. Lillback, *George Washington's Sacred Fire* (Bryn Mawr, PA: Providence Forum Press, 2006), 475. Blackstone's voluminous work on British Common Law begat not only our constitutional framers' ideas of law but also notables such as Abraham Lincoln. Thomas Jefferson borrowed heavily from his understanding of Blackstone as he penned the Declaration of Independence. Blackstone, along with America's jurist giants such as Justices Joseph Story and James Kent, describe Natural Law as that which comes from God himself and a "nature's law" that is always in harmony with God's law.

[110] Ibid., 476.

[111] Caleb Coley, "A Lesson from the Sophists," *Apologetics Press Online,* http://www.apologeticspress.org/APContent.aspx?category=12&article=3525 (accessed February 22, 2013).

[112] The discussion illustrates the question is about whom does a society recognize as authoritative on the subject of morality, God or man? If it is indeed man, then the Air Force leader has embarked upon unchartered waters and an ever-changing sea when determining ethical and moral dilemmas. As man's definition of what is acceptable for behavior changes, so does his morality and value system. This then lends itself to a 'standard' of relativistic truth and political attitudes to determine what is ethical.

[113] Interview with confidential source, October 27, 2012.

[114] Numerous German scientists of Jewish descent found themselves unwelcome in German academic institutions and laboratories. They fled for surrounding countries and many made it to America. This drain of Germany's top intellectual capital had strategic implications and has been documented well by Richard Rhodes. See Richard Rhodes, *The Making of the Bomb* (New York: Simon and Schuster, 1986).

[115] Wester, "Soldier Spirituality," 84.

[116] On December 14, 2012 a gunman walked into Sandy Hook Elementary School in Newtown, CT and killed 20 children and 6 faculty members before killing himself. http://www.cnn.com/2012/12/14/us/connecticut-school-shooting (accessed March 12, 2013).

www.ingramcontent.com/pod-product-compliance
Lightning Source LLC
Chambersburg PA
CBHW080633290526
45790CB00007B/3041